Copyright © 2019 Elizabeth Lutz Pauncz
All Rights Reserved.
No part of this publication may be reproduced, stored in a retrieval system, or transmitted in any form or by any means, electronic, mechanical, photocopying, recording, or otherwise, without permission in writing by the Author.

ISBN 9781079709520

Self Published 2019 in Florence, Italy
www.florencescaravelli.com

Cover: Elizabeth Lutz Pauncz, Jibhi, India 2016

ELIZABETH LUTZ PAUNCZ

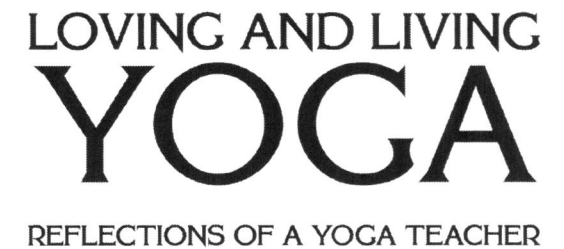

LOVING AND LIVING
YOGA

REFLECTIONS OF A YOGA TEACHER

This book is dedicated to my life-long friends:

Connie Dilley
Bonnie Epstein
Lydia Greenfield
Wallis Wilde Menozzi
Margi Snow

A friend is one of life's greatest gifts.

INTRODUCTION 7

MOVING INTO YOGA 9
The Ocean Garden 10
The Circular Rainbow 11
The Transformative Garden – Comparisons to Yoga 12
The Wave 14
Learning from the Plants 16
The Baby Pose 18
The Story of Two Water Pots 20
Inside Out 22
Bliss 23
Traffic Rush and the Breath 26
Teach to Perfection 28

TAUGHT BY NATURE 29
Human Gardens 30
The Iris on the Compost Heap 32
Gardening as a Child 34
The Hale-Bopp Comet March 1997 36
Winter Sea and Yoga 39
Birds and Fish 40
Lost and Found 42
The Butterfly Theater 43
Carpets and Yoga 45
One 48
Tree Meditation 50
Yoga Outdoors 52

DO YOGA WHEREVER YOU ARE 55
An Imperfect Place to Practice 56
Friendship and Esteem 57
Yoga at Work 58
A Very Simple Breathing Practice 60

TRAVEL — 61

Stone Nests for Plants and What We Can Learn
   from Them — 62
Following Your Dreams — 65
Meditation in Caves — 66
Facing the Dark — 68
A Student's Supposition: Is Yoga Life? — 71
Doors — 73
Flower Grace — 75
Morning Yoga — 77

NEW POSSIBILITIES FOR LEARNING — 79

Quincy Jones — 80
Vanda's Wisdom — 81
Small Things — 84
Food for Thought — 85
Breathing Colors — 86
Mario: Dignity and Hard Work — 89

UNANSWERED QUESTIONS — 91

The How of Why — 92
A Priceless Resource — 95
The God Who Treasures the Less than Perfect — 98
The Turtle Dilemma — 99

ACKNOWLEDGEMENTS — 101

ILLUSTRATIONS — 103

ABOUT THE AUTHOR — 105

INTRODUCTION

Forty-six years ago, I took a summer yoga class at my old high school. I was visiting my parents in Cleveland, having made the long journey from Florence where I lived with my Hungarian husband and our first child. I did not expect to change my life, but from this innocent choice, everything changed. I was drawn deeply into the practice of yoga and, as an immediate sign, I became a vegetarian.

I agree that no one needs to write another technical book on the subject. There are hundreds of excellent texts describing philosophic, historical types of yoga and ways of practice. I, too, as a teacher and student, have written one.

But *Loving and Living Yoga: Reflections of A Yoga Teacher* has not yet been written. It has been waiting for me to overcome my reticence in writing a *sui generis* book, which speaks largely from the personal point of view. I have lived yoga as a practice, but also as a consciousness, where it seems to permeate everyday experience. This state of heightened consciousness or overlap of connection has been called by many names: epiphanies, synchronicities or plainer ones like caring in food preparation. My practice has aided me in recognizing such moments of experiences where meaning is heightened and life shines in a new way or has reinforced positive ideas. For years I have written about these episodes in journals; thus this book is a sharing of personal stories, moments when I lived more intensely or saw more deeply or felt the beauty of existence linked to my being — who I am — because of yoga.

A few notes on my husband, Péter, and my children, Alessandra, who patiently watched as I stood on my head, and Michele, who dutifully obeyed silence while I meditated, appear in this book. The city of Florence, Italy is at times a protagonist. We have lived in three different places since 1963: a residential area, the nearby village of Serpiolle, and the small town of San Domenico, just outside of Florence. Photos and original drawings illustrate and complement the writing.

I have been taught by some of the best teachers in the world. However, when Vanda Scaravelli accepted me as her pupil in 1984, my practice was revolutionised. In the twelve years I was her student and came to understand the three cornerstones of "breath," "wave," and "gravity," my practice changed dramatically. Some of these essays are the outcome of long mornings spent together. Learning was not limited to yoga. This extraordinary humble, wise, and generous woman, who enriched my life and that of many others, will inspire me forever. *Loving and Living Yoga: Reflections of A Yoga Teacher* offers hope and inspiration to every reader through my words, pictures, and drawings.

MOVING INTO YOGA

THE OCEAN GARDEN

I look out at the vast expanse of the ocean that lies before me and it becomes the garden of the world. It is an enormous plot, one that expands out to the sky's farthest edges. As my gaze travels across the infinitesimally small wavelets in constant flux on the calm surface, I pause a moment to reflect on my body. Standing there in reverie, I am drawn within myself. I sense my breath and the beating of my heart and sense the blood as it pulsates. I feel an inexplicable unifying force that meshes with the ever-changing flux of the shifting sea.

Two different currents, one within me and the other beyond, are so close in many ways. My inner self resonates and responds to the gentle wavelets. I am lulled and reassured by something that may not have a name, so deep is its pull.

In this place I am not the gardener but simply one who senses an invisible link to the sea and the myriad of living plants and animals growing in this watery expanse. In this landscape, I am enriched and moved beyond property, care, equipment and toil. I am one with the biggest garden in the world.

THE CIRCULAR RAINBOW

I always thought that rainbows were semi-circles. I suppose this was because I had only seen them from the ground and never from the air. This time it was different, because I was in flight.

The sun was setting and a storm was approaching. And then a rainbow appeared beyond the wing of the plane. It was round, slightly compressed, oblong, and more the color of a neon sign than the traditional colors we are accustomed to. The red was startlingly psychedelic. It made a spectacular brief appearance, disturbing in its intensity, before disappearing again behind the clouds. I was dumbfounded and realized how conditioned we are by our experiences so much so that we fail to imagine the existence of other possibilities such as rainbows that are round.

When landed, the evening storm continued to flash in the distance. Bolts of lightning flew down from the sky, but there was no thunder and just a little rain. The heavens put on a sort of bizarre fireworks show that flashed up and down the horizon for a long time.

THE TRANSFORMATIVE GARDEN - COMPARISONS TO YOGA

Something is always happening in the garden. Watching its activity — growing, changing, going to seed — is fascinating. A small flower may appear or open, seemingly out of nowhere. Perhaps slugs have devoured a plant, leaving only bits and pieces of shredded leaves. Each seed holds its own design for the forth-coming plant; tall, short, robust, spindly, perfectly formed or otherwise.

The longer I teach, the more I realize that, like the seeds in a garden, people come to practice yoga with their own unique bodily design. Some people are extremely flexible; others are quite stiff. Some have delicate necks or challenging spines. There is an infinity of anatomical differences. But now that yoga has become extremely popular, classes are often very large and everyone is expected to do the same thing. It's as if all bodies were made alike, although they are not. Differences are ignored. This practice is regrettable.

Gardens teach me other lessons. Each plant has its own rate of growth and should not be forced. Nature itself sets the rules. This is true for yoga practitioners as well. While a few students can cross their legs from the very beginning, it may take years for others to do so. Forcing only leads to injury, while constant practice and relaxed attempts lead to joyful, healthy, and safe completion of this position.

All gardeners know that patience and acceptance are important attributes for successful gardening. Why shouldn't this apply to yoga as well? A garden transforms itself and is a constant demonstration of the strength of slow progression. The eye needs to be trained to observe this. Our world of modern living and work drives us to move faster. When practicing yoga, transformation is ever present, just like vegetation in the garden, but this may not be evident if our minds are elsewhere and if we are aggressively pushing to reach a goal. Let us take good care of ourselves and trust in nature's lessons and our relaxed bodies' capacities.

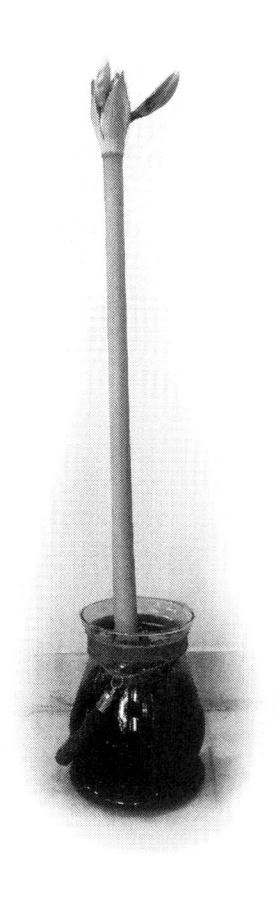

It is strange and slow, but the flower knows it will open beautifully.

THE WAVE

The wave is basic to Vanda's teaching. It is a combination of gravity's downward pull, which is felt in the feet and legs, simultaneously creating an upward supple movement of extension along the spine. There is a corresponding natural opening of the chest. These two powerful forces separate at the back of the waist. With each breath, more and more stability in the lower body is experienced while the upper body becomes lighter and lighter (a feature that is present in all the yoga poses or asanas that we do). The area behind the waist lengthens, and the powerful force of gravity creates space between the vertebrae. When this process is understood and incorporated in your positions, it is relaxing. Vanda often reminded me that elongation and extension could only occur when pulling and pushing ended, and this was the revolution.

The wave cleanses and washes away tensions and impurities. Like the waves in the ocean, it is very strong. In most poses, the movement that one follows is first "down" (to feel the feet making deep contact with the earth) then "up" (the spine straightens and becomes more and more alive) and finally "lift" (as the vertebrae separate before they move in any direction). This entire wave-like process awakens the spine.

This photo was taken when I was in Jibhi, a remote village in Northern India near the border of Tibet, where I went to teach a devoted student. He wanted me to experience a special waterfall and led me there. It was powerful, pure, and magical. Although I was fully dressed and it was rather cold, I began to practice a series of backbends near the falls since it is a good way to experience the wave. As I continued, I found myself drawn into the water under the falls. The cover photo with its double rainbow on the waterfalls, was taken when I was in the water. It was an unforgettable experience!

As water purifies so does the wave:
It takes us into the now of existence.
It refreshes because impurities are eliminated.
It frees.
It is uplifting and when practiced properly, it is a valuable gift that heals the body and sharpens concentration.

Practicing backbends inspired by the falls and "the wave."

LEARNING FROM THE PLANTS

Why do we expect so much from ourselves? Why is there so often a critical voice telling us that "it wasn't good enough," "it was nothing special," "not worth talking about," "not as nice as what someone else knows how to do," etc.? We need to learn from the plants. They do not expect anything in particular from themselves. They grow and lengthen without criticizing themselves constantly. They do not think, "I haven't grown enough," "I'm ugly and not nearly as beautiful as the flower beside me," "It is better than I am."

In the plant world there are many different rates of growth. Cactuses and some palms take years to grow. Does that mean that they are not so successful as a castor oil seed that shoots upward in only a few weeks, towering above all the others with its lovely red-shaded seven-starred leaves, lifting itself to the sky as truthful as an open hand? A bulb, buried dormant in the earth, is invisible. How can we imagine the beauty of the flower that will bloom from it? When things are not going well, instead of blaming ourselves and feeling worthless, could we not say we are in a "bulb stage"? A flower will bloom when there is sun and water and the temperature is right. We should remember that we can become like that too and that, when conditions are right, something unexpected will happen.

Today I did a few of the more difficult yoga postures, which I hadn't tried for several years. Imagine my surprise when I actually enjoyed a stretch that had always been painful, even when I was many years younger. What a delight to find a way of relaxing in what had usually made my muscles cringe.

After decades when that internal critical voice has

often lectured to me, raising my self-doubt, today I heard the voices of the plants, who lovingly encouraged me simply to practice day after day — not seeking something for tomorrow but growing only for today.

As all gardeners know, the soil must be prepared. Even stony ground, with loving attention and the right fertilizer, can become fertile soil. Gardening helps us approach yoga in the right spirit. We need to avoid being influenced by appearances and prepare our soil, knowing that when the moment is right, the flower will boom. The flower is in each one of us. In our own ways, we are all growing beautifully.

*There are many different rates of growth
in the plant world.*

THE BABY POSE —
AND THE MANY WAYS TO RELATE TO IT

This is a very relaxing position that offers a sense of well-being. It resonates in many different ways, as is true of many asanas, when investigated carefully. One day in class, I asked each student to tell us how they experienced the baby pose after having repeated it several times. It was illuminating, because almost every person had a different reaction to the pose.

This led me to realize how differently each person relates to a pose and how little thought is given to the diversity that can be found while doing it. It is fascinating to probe into this kind of question.

Here are some of the observations that were made:

"Resting one's body on the earth is reassuring."

"There is a sense of bowing reverently to the earth."

"By enfolding oneself into this position, a meditative state comes about naturally."

"This position has a double quality: embracing (the earth) implies a component of acceptance of the self."

"There is a reminiscence of being in the safety of the womb: covered and protected by the uterus."

"I don't like to do this pose. My stomach feels cramped, my buttocks don't touch my heels and I can't manage to relax my arms."

"A great benefit is felt by those of us who have painful spinal curvatures. Due to the passive lengthening and opening of the spinal column, I experienced an overwhelming sense of relief."

Almost each person, nonetheless, felt that the pose had led him or her to a profound sense of relaxation. The shape of this position is reminiscent of a snail, a shell, or even an ear: it is a form that is found universally. It creates a resonance without necessitating a definition. Although most people enjoy this position and feel that it is beneficial and relaxing, some do not find it particularly pleasant.

The well-being of a relaxed body is apparent

THE STORY OF TWO WATER POTS*

An elderly Chinese woman had two large pots, each hung on the end of a pole that she carried across her neck. One of the pots had a crack in it, while the other was perfect and always delivered a full portion of water. At the end of the long walks from the stream to the house, the cracked pot arrived only half full. For a full two years this went on daily, with the woman bringing home only one and a half pots of water. Of course, the perfect pot was proud of its accomplishments. But the poor cracked pot was ashamed of its own imperfection and miserable because it could only do half of what it had been made to do.

After two years of what it perceived to be abject failure, it spoke to the woman one day by the stream. "I am ashamed of myself, because this crack in my side causes water to leak out all the way back to your house." The old woman smiled, "Did you notice that there are flowers on your side of the path, but not on the other pot's side? That's because I have always known about your flaw, so I planted flower seeds on your side of the path, and every day while we walk back, you water them. For two years I have been able to pick these beautiful flowers to decorate the table. Without your being just the way you are, there would not be this beauty to grace the house."

*Ancient Chinese fable.

The flawed pot makes the path bright.

INSIDE OUT

A student of mine asked me this question: "Is it true that one of the unique aspects of Vanda Scaravelli's teaching is to move from the inside to the outside? In all the books I have read about yoga, it is always the other way around: one is urged to feel the periphery of the body and to go more and more inside."

Vanda often pointed out that gravity allows muscles to work correctly. They respond "like magnets attracted to the earth" and following gravity's pull, they lengthen, relax, and awaken as a result. This force originates from within and moves towards the periphery. Squeezing or contracting muscles may be considered an outward movement (going from out to in). It is the wrong direction because it creates rigidity.

Vanda taught that when you are practicing an asana, you should exhale. There are numerous reasons for this: as you exhale, the spine naturally lengthens. In exhalation, your abdomen is moving inward towards the spine without any forcing on your part. As a result, the spine is awakened. In exhalation, air is released from your body: this is a purifying process and an invitation to release tensions. If you are mentally in tune with your body, you are led into a distillation and elimination of accumulated debris: there is a ridding of many things that have built up over the years — damaging or misunderstood thoughts, incorrect body positioning, erroneous actions, etc. Therefore, moving from inside out is correct.

BLISS

When my third grandchild was born, my daughter-in-law asked me what it means to be a grandmother. I am still thinking about the answer. Many grandparents say that they are happy not to have the responsibility of raising children once again, but I have never agreed with this sentiment. It has been a great privilege to watch my grandchildren grow and to bond with them. One benefit of growing old is finding time, in spite of a busy and engaged life, to keep them company without feeling stressed. Parents, on the other hand, are constantly having to manage a balancing act between their work, preparing meals, negotiating sibling fights, supervising homework, and driving their kids to countless activities. Usually I can relate to my grandchildren in a yoga-like way. Years of practice have forged strength, commitment, and decision, as well as studying at the school of life. I can usually pay close attention to my grandchildren and listen with patience without being in a hurry. As a result, being in their presence gives me deep satisfaction.

Gurus have offered many instructions about ways to attain bliss. They are all very complicated and quite discouraging. My version of "bliss," however, is very down to earth. It does not involve sitting rigidly or practicing severe austerities but rather staying alert to the multitude of special moments that occur every day in which contentment, happiness, and perhaps, bliss, can be glimpsed.

Of course we are all different, so the ways of finding this sort of elation are varied. Pleasure can be found in a variety of simple every day events: taking the dog for a walk and reveling in one of its silly antics; smiling at a stranger when an unspoken look of comprehension is exchanged; watching children and seeing their innocence and amazement; experiencing a sunset. These are only a few ways that we can travel effortlessly into the house of well-being.

Last year, I was with my grandson, Dario, at the sea sailing on an inflatable boat. As he observed nature, the sea, the sky, and the birds flying overhead, his face expressed marvel, and an unspoken understanding passed between us. This was enough to put me into the happiest state imaginable.

Dario and Grandma at the sea

Dario's sister, Lisa, is an actress. She had the lead in the film, *Girl in Flight*. I had the privilege to be her parental guardian for a week in Rome. It was an experience I will never forget. I loved being close to her and admiring her maturity and talent from the sidelines. I saw a side to her personality that I had never imagined. It was a great thrill.

Daniel, their younger cousin, never stops playing. He is very serious about his games. I am elated when he tells me that I am a princess, and even when the game is over that is still my role.

Lisa and me on her film set

Last week, I looked up and saw a double rainbow. I was totally unprepared for the moment it gave me. This spontaneous second of deep satisfaction is something that is there, available for all of us if we simply stop for a moment and look around. Yoga teaches us to slow down, wake up to our surroundings, and experience the wonders of the world. Call it instant happiness, contentment, or bliss.

TRAFFIC RUSH AND THE BREATH

Florence was not built for cars. A few streets are still cobbled with centuries-old, massive, basalt blocks. Others are paved with small hand-cut stone "bricks" called "little Saint Peters," artistically set in a lovely fan pattern in the shape of a peacock tail, a design that has been passed down from antiquity. The main street leading from the station to the Duomo is a good example of this. These streets are extremely hazardous. Many of our streets are narrow and treacherous, due to parked cars that create an obligatory one-way system.

Since the traffic situation is so bad, many people travel on motorbikes, scooters, or bicycles. Doctors, workers, professionals, students, and sales people make up a frightening number of two-wheel daredevils who think nothing of passing on either the left or right. Young riders, who can drive scooters at the age of fourteen and have little road sense, love to dart in and out of cars that are in motion, especially the boys, fueled by testosterone. Not surprisingly, there are many bad accidents. Driving a car takes strong nerves, a cool head, and fast reflexes. Keeping one's temper is very difficult.

Another challenge is that the roads can be free or jammed. As a result, the time it takes to get to my studio can range from seven minutes to half an hour. Trying to predict the flow of traffic is next to impossible, and this leads to great stress.

One of the few antidotes that I have found is to practice simple breathing, concentrating on the air as it enters my lungs and then releasing it, to empty them completely. I need to keep my mind disengaged and calm so as not to get trapped into worrying about getting to my destination on time. Focusing on my breath entering and exiting through my nose is also important. After a few minutes, my breathing takes over and braking or accelerating becomes a secondary and natural process. Of course, my hands stay firmly placed on the wheel and my eyes never leave the road, but they are relaxed, as are my shoulders. Steady calm breathing is the only way I know to buck traffic and remain serene.

TEACH TO PERFECTION

Vanda readjusted my body so it would be able to respond more fully thanks to the directions of her hands or feet. She was a master at communicating through touch and example. Her words were always few, succinct, and direct. She took each pupil to her maximum possibilities. It was a slow process to lead her selected students to see a glimmer of what she had discovered. There was never a time when she didn't do her utmost to take each of us to new heights of understanding. The profundity of her teaching is often misinterpreted. It is subtle and demanding.

One time when Vanda was doing a position at eighty-six, she turned to me with a smile and said, "I am getting better." Her insistence on precision and excellence and her dignified, unrelenting communication of being *au point* (to use her words), has enabled me to get closer to comprehending her revolutionary way of practicing.

Teachers must teach students to perfection. That is we must perfect ourselves, not the students. Why is it that yoga teachers often have a need to feel superior? Those of us who have more experience should help younger teachers. We could reassure them by admitting that all of us have had doubts and that there are times when we question what we are doing. Being able to "perform" a position perfectly is not a license to feel proud or "successful," in my opinion. Nor does having large numbers of students prove very much.

TAUGHT BY NATURE

HUMAN GARDENS

Plants have their own sense of time and show us how to nurture patience. We humans are used to planning, getting, doing, and finishing up and perhaps give little thought to the different rhythms of the life that surrounds us. Many seeds teach me a different lesson. They germinate in God's time, and that may be slow. Sometimes it seems impossible that there could be any life at all in a seed or bulb that has not yet sprouted in what seems like dormant soil, but then I remember the comment a professional gardener made when I complained that a plant was very frustrating in its almost negligible growth.

"Five years in gardening time," he said "is really very little."

Yoga, likewise, is similar for many of us. There are some positions that seem impossible, but, with constant effort and painstaking practice, one can make very slow progress in a difficult asana, and in time it can become one that is done with pleasure.

What would it be like if we were to consider our bodies and minds as special gardens? There may be some vegetation in our yoga garden that seems barren and unpromising, but there are many undreamed-of possibilities that, just like plants, may take a long time to emerge.

This analogy does not only apply to a progressive development and understanding of yoga: all of life's experiences may be considered a human garden. Growth is nourished by inspiration in various forms—such as a significant piece of music, a favorite poem, a special painting, the dear voice of a child, or the unforgettable smile of a lover. Paradoxically, the ache of a sorrow may also nourish, transform, and ripen the soil of the soul.

Each of us lives in his or her own garden, although we may forget and neglect our great underestimated resources.

THE IRIS ON THE COMPOST HEAP

My garden is really a cypress woods, and my friends warned me that "nothing grows under cypress trees," but, having lived in the city for twenty-two years, I was hungry to grow plants and flowers, so I paid little heed to those admonitions.

One sloping hill was covered in wild irises that were relatively healthy but never bloomed. My gardening books advised digging them up and replanting the strongest part of the root. I set to work, pulling up hundreds of spent and unpromising plants, moving some of the best ones to a sunnier spot, and fertilizing them. The following spring, the experiment proved to be a miserable failure. None of the pampered and cared-for plants ever bloomed.

One day, as I was throwing away some leaves on a makeshift compost pile, I accidentally discovered one iris that was in bloom. The only flower in the entire woods was a reject I had thrown away! It veered out to one side, slanting like the Tower of Pisa, showing its lovely purple petals and yellow tongue, blooming in the shadiest, most forlorn and forsaken part of the property.

We have no control over how things grow. There are invisible laws at work, and plants, like humans, develop where and how they want to. As with the iris, we are totally ignorant of the hidden reasons for undreamed-of success; nor is there any explanation for failures in spite of skill, investment of time, and special preparations.

It veered out like The Tower of Pisa.

GARDENING AS A CHILD

I think I have always been a gardener. When I was six years old, I had my first garden. In the years during and after the Second World War, Americans were encouraged to raise their own vegetables to help save money and boost the economy. Many schools designated a part of their grounds as gardening areas, which were plowed, leaving enormous chunks of ugly barren upturned earth. As a small child, I had no knowledge about these things and signed up for the 8:00 a.m. gardening session. Three times a week, I woke up early in the morning and walked over to the school grounds to begin my gardening experience.

Every gardener or early riser knows the unique quality of the early morning hours. The quiet and peace of the morning light and the smell of the grass and earth were simply part of me. It is good to be young and live this sensation. As we grow older, we lose this natural, peaceful communion and we become divided into many compartments.

Gardening as a child was hard work but I don't remember thinking in those terms at the time. Each young gardener was given a cultivator to break down the sun-baked clay soil in order to prepare her very own plot. When this task was finished, brown paper bags of seeds were produced. A few seeds were counted out into our small open palms, entrusting us with those magical lives. I particularly recall the feel and smell of the white bean seeds, shiny, large and encouraging in their positive presence. Corn, too, with its bumpy yellow hard kernels was fascinating. Several weeks after our seeds were distributed, we were given young eggplants, tomatoes, and squash to be transplanted into our gardens. I never felt that we received quite enough of them to fill out the empty spaces, but in those times an unspoken Protestant frugality lay behind a great deal of our lives. My parents, in fact, never failed to remind us how hard it had been to live through the Great Depression. Their subtle remarks surely influenced our young lives.

After four years of gardening, I was surprised one August day to be told that I was to be awarded a golden pin in recognition of my faithful gardening. I had no idea that such a thing existed, since gardening had become special in its own right. The satisfaction that I received in gardening was a reward in itself.

There are some parallels in our approach to yoga. Vanda's approach to yoga addresses this very issue. Body and mind come peacefully together through breath, wave and gravity and we practice for the pleasure of it and for the satisfaction it gives us. I had been practicing seriously for 12 years and had mastered some very difficult positions, but relaxation and enjoyment had no place in the way I was taught. My life changed forever when I became one of Vanda's students and practiced individually with her once a week for years. At first, her approach to yoga was alien to me: "No motivation, no aims, only an agreeable appointment for the body to look forward to. We do it for the fun of it." (*Awakening the Spine*, 2012 edition, p. 15). It took me several years to understand how to work hard while staying relaxed at the same time. Gradually, I discovered a new agreeable aspect of my personality and found practicing in this precious new way a reward in itself, much like gardening had been for me as a child.

THE HALE-BOPP COMET
MARCH 1997: FOUR DIFFERENT VIEWINGS

The Hale-Bopp comet will not come again for another 2,500 years. It was the brightest of our century, one thousand times brighter than Halley's. I was able to experience its magic in Italy for an entire month.

The first night I sighted the comet, the weather was agreeable and the sky clear. It appeared on the northwest horizon, directly below Cassiopeia, and was like nothing I had ever seen before. Its uniqueness was exciting beyond words, and it kindled an archaic reawakening of knowledge and recognition that transcended thought. As I gazed at the sky and marveled at how quickly it was passing, I tried to imagine how the people thousands of years ago might have related to this remarkable phenomenon. What kind of an explanation would they have given? Might it have been "the star of wonder, star of light" of the three wise kings from the Orient? How would the Egyptians have explained the comet? We are unable to access that part of emotional history, which is lost but not entirely forgotten.

After gazing for some time in subdued reverie, I returned home slightly shaken and sat in meditation, which helps process emotions in moments such as these.

The next occasion for viewing was at 5 a.m. The comet had moved to the northeastern sky not far from the constellation of Taurus. Unique and solitary, it traveled majestically through the sky, its veil of icy gaseous masses trailing behind. The moment was pure magic. The flowers of Queen Anne's Lace in the field like small boats on a black firmament of grass, the moon sinking in red hues on the western horizon, exactly opposite the spot where the sun would soon rise, and the hooting of an owl in the distance, ushered in this very special Palm Sunday of March 23, 1997.

I felt extraordinarily blessed to be alive in this moment and went back home to sit, once again, practicing *Pranayama* far into the bright light of morning.

A group of yoga students joined me for the next viewing on a very cold night. The astrophysicists of Arcetri (just outside Florence) had mounted telescopes on a nearby mountain, appropriately named Battidenti or "Teeth Chatterer." We waited our turn to view the comet. Hale-Bopp seen through the telescope was disappointing, because only the enlarged nucleus was in focus. Still, it was fascinating to see it being pushed around by its dissolving parts. The queen of the night, however, was the first quarter of the moon, shockingly bright - so much so that it seemed as if some kind of enormous light had been turned on behind it. Magnification revealed undreamed of craters. The barely distinguishable perfect round circle was astonishingly outlined. Its portion, mysterious in hidden elusiveness, contrasted starkly against the bright one. I could understand the beguiling nature and fascination that the moon has wielded throughout the centuries.

My final viewing of Hale-Bopp was a fleeting adieu. There had been many cloudy nights when it had been impossible to see the comet. Soon it would no longer be visible, as it was much lower on the horizon. The city of Florence is nestled in the valley surrounded by hills and mountains. The comet moved very quickly. Its nucleus sank like a dazzling sun beyond the horizon, but its trail lasted for many minutes. It looked like a misty cloudy geyser spouting into the sky for what seemed like an endless amount of time.

Suspension of future and past,
forgotten because of the wonder of the universe,
found me enveloped in awe of the pageantry of the night.
I was lost, drawn into the silent movement of eternity
ticking by in the moment of the most real now.

WINTER SEA AND YOGA

For many years my family went to Viareggio, a well-known seaside resort not far from Florence, so that my husband, Péter, could play bridge in a national tournament. After we had settled into our hotel, we decided to take a walk on the pier, which extends far out onto the sea. The day was overcast and the colors of the shimmering waters changed from dark jade to muted grey to deep bottle green. There was movement everywhere, and the water seemed to have a life of its own. This vast space was strangely reassuring in its silence and drama.

Behind us were ominous banks of dark rain clouds that were quickly piling up over the Apuan Mountains where the famous marble quarries lie. The sea was murky but near the horizon a shiny silver line where the sky touched the sea was infused with dazzling back lighting from the invisible sun. For a few brief minutes the rays of the sun streamed down overhead through the clouds so that beams of soft light descended earthward, resting on the gentle deep-turquoise waves. The colors were winter ones and they exuded a deep sense of peace and beauty that lifted my spirits into an appreciation of the infinitesimal gradations of their dark somber hues offering a greater variety of tones than could ever be found on a bright sunny day.

It was an expanding moment that was painted and stored in each of my cells. The practice of yoga can be a way to develop an appreciation of "what is" and to discover internal space. Stretching and extending body to brain and muscle to spine, lead us, as the sky extends to the sea, to a source where there is calm and peacefulness. This nourishing of spirit, which offers a silent plenitude of grace, is an emotion that any of us can experience if we submit to time and breath.

BIRDS AND FISH

I treasure the bird population and delight in the migratory movements of nature's unfolding seasonal orchestration. Today, in Cleveland, the sky was steel grey. From the north, flying like perfectly trained acrobatic planes, black geese from Canada appeared in a perfect V formation. Each one flew in flawless harmony with the others. Their long black necks majestically set off the split-second coordination of their grey wings, which followed a deep but unheard beat. Then, faster than thought, the V turned into a long straight single line as one of the two strongest lead fliers flipped through the air, turning over and upside down while the other one, protecting the weakest, brought up the rear. Chaos had seemingly shaken out all order; however, the geese unexpectedly dropped perfectly onto a lagoon. No airplane formation could have been nearly this beautiful, nor could it have moved so quickly and efficiently as those large Canadian geese, who in perfect synchronization, followed a grander design than anyone could imagine.

Why are we, the most evolved of the animal kingdom, so far behind in heeding the moves of others?

Why can't we, who certainly follow the same plan unknowingly, live with this beautiful social awareness?

Each of us, like the birds, is a single being but only one small part of a much greater order.

While I was swimming in the transparent blue waters of Calabria near a large porous wall that extended into the profundity of the sea, my eye fell upon hundreds of miniscule iridescent azure fish. Their sudden appearance was as shocking as touching blue lightning while spotting a three dimensional hologram of small arrows in movement.

The sun blazed down, dividing the water into layers of shimmering colors; bright azure, dazzling emerald, dove grey, translucent white. All were mixed together by the palette of the sea.

In this watery dimension where time and space dissolve into infinity, the small wondrous blue inhabitants thrilled me. Their capacity to glide or streak in perfect accord, depending on mysterious invisible signals, always amazes me. There is a silent harmony and peacefulness that they transmit as a group. Each single blue soul, separate but at the same time totally interdependent, rewards and fascinates the silent observer.

LOST AND FOUND

If you don't get lost, there's a chance you may never be found. *Author Unknown*

There comes a time in one's life when some kind of an experience (a death, an unwanted change of home, a job loss, an unexpected health issue) comes as such a jolt that we lose touch with who we thought we were. Everything seems out of place, and the certainties that made up a part of our self-identity are no longer there.

We feel lost.
Questions arise:
Who am I?
What is the meaning of my existence?
What is happening and why?

This is a moment that necessitates "holding" and "calm abiding" and, no matter what, not giving up but finding a way to trust something much larger than we had imagined.

Life itself.

In time, a beautiful sunrise will appear on the horizon. The adage of "losing oneself to find oneself" or of "letting go" may become an unexpected reality. Of all the things that the Dalai Lama has said, the one I love the most is: "Never give up."
Those words are a little boat that carries us across the great waters.

THE BUTTERFLY THEATER

There are many different kinds of butterflies here in the country. One kind is particularly impressive because it looks like a miniature parachute with large white wings that gradually taper into almost nothing, making it look very much like it is wearing a small pair of pants. Black etching along its fluted wings dramatically turns into a thin dark line.

As I looked out of the window one morning, two of these special creatures put on a spectacular exhibition of dancing and movement with the entire Arno Valley as a backdrop.

Taking its cue from an invisible director, one butterfly would come "on stage" and sail across the sky. Then following some precise but unfathomable timing, the other would appear to meet its partner in mid-air. At times they almost touched, then they twirled in a complex and intriguing *pas-de-deux* dropping into a vortex of ever-turning movement. Suddenly one would take off and run across the sky playing a frantic elegant game of hide and seek. One player would disappear while the other would move into rapid flight, searching for its lost partner. A kind of jet-timed tag continued as both wove beautifully through the air, stopping occasionally to land on a flower to sip some nectar. It was a breathtaking performance, a symphony without sound and a communion of the absolute held on the airy stage of the universe.

There are moments in every life when we are replenished by some unexpected and surprising event such as this "performance." We may be feeling rather dismal and discouraged and the event can cheer our spirits. Yoga has this capacity as well. At times, we may start out forlorn and dispirited, but then somehow, miraculously, our bodies respond unexpectedly and give us a gift of grace that can carry us through difficult moments.

They played an elegant game of tag.

CARPETS AND YOGA

A dear friend of ours left us some very special rugs that were family heirlooms. They were in need of repair and needed to be washed as well. There is a special technique involved that is labor-intensive and expensive. As a consequence, I decided to try and clean them on my own. I began with a small strip, filling up the bathtub, scrubbing, and rinsing, and finally hauling the very heavy wet rug outside to dry on a sizzling summer day. It was as heavy as a six year old. The end result came out very well, and the colors were extraordinary.

All of the other rugs needing to be washed were much bigger, and I felt quite desperate, until I remembered that rugs are very sturdy and not easily damaged, and that, in the past, they were washed outside in rivers. So one by one, I carried the big rugs outside onto a very large space in front of the house, which is paved with slabs of flagstone. I scrubbed each of them section by section on my hands and knees, rinsing them with the garden hose and using my bare feet to finish the final cleaning. I began to feel a connection to unknown elder sisters at rivers doing the same thing in far away countries and, although it was fatiguing work, a kind of vibrant energy overtook me. We were outside, sun on our backs, water on our feet, washing and cleaning, acts that women have performed for centuries.

It was a very strange sight to see those beautiful rugs laid outside. They seemed to become friendly and alive as I hauled them around, moving them from one torrid stone to another. I honestly felt that they were happy. The darkest rug, too, freed from decades of dirt, glowed in the sun as did the others - priceless jewels of an ancient tradition.

While I was scrubbing, I was able to practice a yoga position that involves squatting and positioning the heels completely flat on the ground. In this asana, *Malanasana* (the garland pose), your arms reach around behind your back and your hands catch each other. It has always been extremely difficult for me to get my heels completely on the ground and in contrast to my graceful eighty-nine-year-old teacher, I feel like a big awkward donkey whenever I try this asana. Nonetheless, as I scrubbed for hours, I continued to work on getting my heels to touch the ground and properly position my bent legs. This demanding asana improved tremendously since I practiced it over and over, and the experience proved to me that yoga in action keeps work meaningful.

Practicing yoga while washing the rug

ONE

I have a fond memory of my grandfather's lovely back yard with raspberries climbing up a white picket fence at the end of his garden. Inspired by this memory and stubbornly ignoring the reality of inadequate growing conditions, I decided to plant six raspberry bushes. I needed to create an area and clear away overgrowth and rocks to prepare the soil. I dug holes using a hoe, pick axe, and shovel. It was exhausting work.

Only one bush took root. I visited this little wonder several times a day to watch its progress, somewhat like a mother who checks her baby. This lonely bush had only one slender branch with just six, small, bell-like flowers dangling daintily from it. After more than a month, six small ripe, red fruits were ready to be eaten.

I never "feasted" on more than one berry on any given day. Plucking this tiny fruit was a ritual that lasted several minutes. First, I observed the undersized red, clustered seeds of the berry enveloped in soft juiciness. Then it found its way into my mouth. Of course I didn't begin to chew it immediately but rather sucked on it very slowly. Savoring became a kind of meditation.

The curious thing I discovered is that one of my raspberries was the equivalent of a whole bowlful of store-bought ones. Only one berry was totally satisfying.

Why was that? How could just one small berry satisfy me? Was it the attentive eye, having watched the slow development of the fruit, that somehow nourished me? Or could it be the love and toil of raising this plant that fed me more than food? Or was it the undivided attention I gave to the ritual of eating?

There were only six soft berries.

TREE MEDITATION

Tree meditation is an ancient practice that is predominant in many religious traditions. It is most helpful in balancing energy and activating the creative force that is in each of us. Sai Baba said it is one of the most effective meditations in existence.

Sit in a quiet spot in the lotus position, half lotus or whatever other position is comfortable. Imagine your favorite tree or visualize any other beautiful majestic tree that comes to mind. Give yourself time to inspect it attentively. See the branches above you, rising to the sky. These branches represent divine male energy. Picture the enormous roots that symbolize divine nourishing feminine strength. Can you see the roots?

Inhale, imagine that you are pulling energy into your body through the large system of leaves and branches. Exhale deeply. This expelled air is clearing impurities and removing stagnated debris. The law of physics states that when a void is created (by emptying the lungs), it is replaced by something else (fresh air). The divine male energy that is pulled in from above through your leaves, invigorates and renews. Once you begin to have this sensation, switch to your roots.

Visualize the roots growing deeply into the earth. They mirror the branches. See them in your mind's eye. This energy is Yin (as opposed to the celestial Yang). As you inhale, pull in stabilizing nutrient energy from your roots. Again, as before, breathe out all that is unneeded. As you inhale, every cell of your body is replenished and revitalized.

When there is a steady flow of air, you are ready for the final step, which is to breathe through your countless leaves and deep roots simultaneously, allowing the new energies to mix when you inhale, and to release old stale impurities when you exhale.

Free yourself through breathing. If you practice regularly, power spontaneously flows through you, and you will discover the harmony and perfection of your own being.

Imagine your favorite tree or visualize one.

YOGA OUTDOORS

Yoga outside is such an experience! It is very refreshing and regenerating but it can also be distracting. The pull of nature is overpowering and the vastness of the outdoors is disorienting compared to the enclosed space of a room. In the first years when I practiced outside, I realized that doing so took quite a lot of concentration.

If there are trees, there is almost always a constant fluttering of leaves, each with a different rhythm and movement. The wind ruffles them and each branch gracefully sways in its own way. Nature is so healing and restorative.

Today I am standing under some umbrella pine trees, which are typically found in Tuscany. The needles under my yoga mat become soft messengers to my feet. I wait for several minutes in *Tadasana* (the mountain pose), standing still with active feet and a straight, relaxed body. What a blessing it is to have feet as sensitive as ears and "hear" the carpet that I am standing on. Thousands of long, horizontally flattened dried needles underfoot put me in contact with the tender earth. It is such a special, beautiful moment.

I take my time and breathe. All worries, all thoughts slowly dissolve. Now I feel ready to do something more challenging. A nearby bench invites me to try *Halasana* (the plow posture). It is quite narrow, and that offers just enough difficulty to make for an interesting exercise.

By taking time to listen carefully, your body will tell you what to do and you may surprise yourself by doing positions that you hadn't thought of. On the other hand, there could come an invitation to sit and practice

Pranayama (breathing). The most important thing, in this case, is to sit comfortably: perhaps in *Vajarasana* (sitting on your heels), simple half crossed legs, or *Padmasana* (the lotus pose), etc.

There may not be many opportunities to practice outside. Each day is an experience to be savored and enjoyed. Each is precious. The sun, air, and earth are elements that strengthen and prepare us for the coming months.

**DO YOGA
WHEREVER
YOU ARE**

AN IMPERFECT PLACE TO PRACTICE

Often, as yogis, we seek a quiet isolated place to practice, as suggested by Patanjali. What happens if you do not find yourself in such ideal conditions? Do you stop practicing? No, of course not. You begin to practice by not yielding to distractions and drawing inward into heightened awareness of your breath and finding stability in your body.

I am in Hungary without a yoga mat. I have improvised by using a towel. There is a miniscule balcony outside my room. Yogis can make themselves small, so that problem is resolved.

There are noises of all sorts: the old-fashioned yellow trams screech on their tracks, blue stream-lined buses stop and go, cars honk, and motorcycles rev their motors. Is this disturbing? Yes, of course. Do I stop practicing? No, of course not. Visible from my perch is the flowing Danube, a working river. Barges, small ships, ferries, and sightseeing boats — all move incessantly along this majestic river. Their movements are sure and quiet. Finally, I remind myself that the Buddha was at ease meditating in the market place, and I draw on this knowledge to hone my skills of living and practicing in the everyday world.

Living and practicing in Budapest in the everyday world

FRIENDSHIP AND ESTEEM

Vanda Scaravelli and B.K.S. Iyengar have been instrumental in proposing new ways to approach yoga. The two were great friends. Both Mr. Iyengar and T.K.V. Desikachar adored Vanda. She was extremely generous in helping both men and at the same time enormously humble.

I would like to share a very sweet moment when Mr. Iyengar was visiting Vanda at her home in Fiesole. He wanted to see how her backbends looked (I don't think he had seen her do yoga in many years). She was not at all in agreement and tried to dissuade him, but he insisted. It might come as a surprise to learn that he evaluated her backbends in her small kitchen. She was preparing some food, as was often her way, but right then and there he had her do a backbend over the washing machine.

It was a demonstration of simplicity and directness as well as proof that yoga is with us every minute and in any place.

Vanda Scaravelli with B.K.S. Iyengar

YOGA AT WORK

I received a wonderful surprise in the mail. It was a calendar for the coming year with the most inviting photos of yoga in action. Each month a person dressed in normal clothes was featured doing a yoga position in his or her workplace. Where did Anna and Wolfi find such an inspired idea?

It is truly yoga working even at work.

Each photo reveals someone like you and me demonstrating how even a few minutes of practice in the workplace can improve life. There is no need to change clothes or use a yoga mat. Each page of the calendar is a reminder and an invitation just to do it.

The story continues and gets even better. This inspired idea came about not only to encourage us all to practice, anywhere and anytime — even for a few minutes — but, equally important, it was created to raise funds for the creation of a hospice, which is badly needed in East Suffolk (located about two hours from London). All profits from the calendar will go to the hospice-building fund.

Rebecca at her bakery

A VERY SIMPLE BREATHING EXERCISE

Yoga comes to the rescue when done peacefully and with unswerving attention to the breath. Yoga schools are as varied as a flower garden filled with many species that fill it with a riot of colors.

I would like to share a way to practice *Pranayama*. There are no special techniques to follow: by focusing exclusively on inhalation and exhalation you can automatically slow down your nervous system.

This can be done by anyone, independent of age or health. It is deceptively simple:

> Sit quietly and concentrate on the air as it fills your lungs when inhaling.
> Maintain awareness as air is slowly emptied out in exhalation.
> Do this for at least five minutes.

When you have finished and before changing positions, try looking inside yourself. Thoughts may arise:

> What made me unhappy about a recent discussion?
> What do I really need to do today?
> What is actually important?

There are countless thoughts within us.

Solutions to problems may spontaneously present themselves. Some of them may seem trivial, but they may offer real relief.

Any positive thoughts will be of benefit to yourself and others.

TRAVEL

STONE NESTS FOR PLANTS AND WHAT WE CAN LEARN FROM THEM

It was Christmas. Alessandra and Luciano were in Pakistan visiting friends, and Michele was in Mexico. The thought of passing the holidays without them seemed too dreary for holiday cheer, and I asked my travel agent for a suggestion, since Péter and I are always interested in sunny places near the sea. She proposed the Canary Islands.

Lanzerote, the most easterly of the seven major islands just off the coast of Africa, lies 100 kilometers west of the Sahara Desert. It looked like an interesting destination. This island, with its more than 300 extinct volcanoes, was saved from high-rise buildings and monotonous tourist hotels by the vision and insistence of César Manrique, a famous architect born on the island, who wrote that "to be absolutely free to create without fear or formula heartens the soul and opens a path to the joy of living." The island reflects his spirit.

Much of the island is sparsely vegetated, and natural flora has advanced slowly over thousands of years, first putting forth lichens, moss and a few long reeds waving here and there in the winds that sweep across the ever-present dark rocks. In some areas, the landscape is as forlorn as the surface of the moon.

The inhabitants, with enormous toil and great love, have fitted out an individual nest called *La Geria* for each plant. First they portion off their plot by erecting low stone walls with the volcanic rocks collected from their property and from the nearby mountains. Then they spread black lava cinders over the rocky fields, making a smooth bed. Finally, they build small circular partitions for each individual vine in their vineyards.

They use the same system for cacti, which they raise to capture cochineal beetles, which are dried and ground into a powder to be used as a medicinal drug, for dye, or for food coloring. They tenderly place each plant within these small semi-circular walls, creating a shield that protects each one from the trade winds. The black volcanic ash absorbs night dew from the atmosphere. It is exactly the right temperature to nourish each plant. But I think the strongest element for growth must come from the tender care and attention that the inhabitants constantly give to each individual plant.

I began to realize that there are some parallels between these arduous preparations and a serious yoga practice. Bodies need special attention and care when first approaching the study of yoga, just like the preparation of the nests. Many people are stiff, and even sitting on the floor in a "comfortable" position, is quite demanding for them. With perseverance, week after week, something similar to smoothing out the lava cinders begins to occur. It takes work and dedication to prepare the body slowly for positions that will be assumed easily in some future time. The first year may necessitate something close to a leap of faith for some people to believe that things will improve over time, as many have neglected their physical well-being for years. Dedication is needed, much like that necessary to tend the plants. The night dew that benefits them is similar to our restful breathing that absorbs fresh air, soaking it in from the atmosphere.

Across these terraced fields, the patterns were reminiscent of Inca designs. A donkey pulled a simple plow, while a farmer planted sweet potatoes in the dark receptive soil. Perhaps it is not such an impossible leap of the imagination to see the affinities between this culture and the Incas: two ancient cultures, both based on attachment to the earth and reverence for the power of nature.

There is great primordial knowledge behind this slow, humble work that weds humankind to the earth and universe. We are lost in a morass of cities far from the heavenly touch of the open sun, worlds away from the force of strong, reassuring earth, where pure and fresh breezes sweep, majestic and mysterious, in a silent song touching everyone. Reflecting on this and the differences in our lives and theirs, I remember that we can help ourselves greatly by stopping during the day to relax and breathe for a few minutes.

Let us practice together: quietly take a few peaceful breaths and feel the reassuring force of gravity, as our feet make full contact with the floor. Visualize a lovely, tranquil scene. The power of peace and light leads us to a long-forgotten safe place. A few more breaths will invigorate us, bringing joy to this special moment. When we return to our activities, we are refreshed.

FOLLOWING YOUR DREAMS

"Follow your dreams" is an adage that reminds us of realistic possibilities. Since olden times, there have been those who listened to their dreams and placed importance on the messages they received during the night. If we pay close attention to our dreams, rich information unfolds for us. It is a free gift from our psyche.

There is so much static in our minds, however, that dreams may soon be forgotten or be confusing to understand. We get thrown into our busy lives and forget about our deep nights' lessons.

We might find an entrance into our "dream world" before we start to practice. Instead of beginning with asanas, we can breathe quietly and let our limbs settle down and rest so they can restore themselves. The soul expands and speaks through silence, clearing a path, so that precious information from the dream world can reveal itself.

Do not dismiss any idea or intuition as impossible. The universe is waiting to respond to a dream suggestion. Believe in yourself and act. This will set into motion new possibilities that may really make your dreams come true.

MEDITATION IN CAVES

My first introduction to a cave was when I was quite young. My father, who was very adventurous, took us to Old Man's Cave in Southern Ohio. He had to carry me across the rushing water to get to the entrance. The experience was quite scary. I still remember viewing the blind fish in a small pond inside the cave.

When I began to do yoga, my interest in caves changed somewhat. Meditating inside one, undeniably offers special energy. Is it the darkness? The enclosed protected space? The constant temperature? Vibrations? Emanations? Each meditator probably has his or her own explanation.

The photo below indicates the struggle I had to get through the small entryway of Wasusta Cave outside of Rishikesh where Sivananda meditated. Once inside, I was amazed to dimly glimpse a sadhu, (a Hindu ascetic, who has renounced worldly life), bound to silence, sitting motionlessly. We sat together for some time. There are other memorable caves that I have experienced: Arunachala in Tamil Nadu (where Ramana meditated), Mt Abu in Rajasthan (where a confounded sadhu found his place taken), the Queen's Chamber in the Great Pyramid at Giza, and a small one I happened upon at the sea in Italy.

Your cave is waiting for you somewhere. If you have already found it, you can always return there by calling it into your mind's eye. And so you can meditate in that special space at any time.

Looking somewhat like Winnie the-Pooh

FACING THE DARK

Any year, before I plan to take a yoga group abroad, I travel by myself to discover places that have special energy and seem appropriate. Tamil Nadu in India was unique in many ways, and in those days long before the availability of internet, I poured over The Lonely Planet for months, hunting for good destinations.

I was strongly attracted to the Matrimandir in Auroville, a special center for meditation that The Mother was having built. (She and Sri Aurobindo were spiritual teachers in nearby Pondicherry). Her vision was to create a peaceful place for the benefit of all mankind. As a result, her disciples undertook its construction in a barren and poverty-stricken area that she had chosen.

I booked a room that was the closest I could find to the Matrimandir so I could meditate there every day. Upon arrival, I left my bag, asked for directions and took a bike and a map. I am sure it is different now, but then there were only dirt paths and no signs. Following my map with some difficulty and asking an occasional passerby, I arrived at a long woodsy path that ended in a large open area. The huge sphere of the Matrimandir, still under construction, was being covered with enormous golden discs. The structure was impressive and elaborate.

I approached respectfully and for some reason was allowed entrance, although the afternoon had been assigned to meditators who lived in this community. Entering quietly, I encountered a special silence, quieter than silence itself, that reigned within. The dazzling white interior was spacious. Devotees dressed in white were absorbed in inward concentration. A giant glass globe hung down in the center, reflecting light that streamed in from above. Not a word was spoken. Time disappeared.

Much later, our deep reverie came to its conclusion. Very large white sheets were brought out, and the areas where morning meditators would sit began to be covered. I was asked to participate in this ritual and felt overwhelmed by the privilege of being included. When we had finished, before I realized what was happening, everyone had gone. I was alone and was left to try to find the way to my bike.

The Matrimandir as it looked when I was there

An even greater surprise awaited me when I opened the door. I encountered pitch-black open space, blacker than night itself. This darkness was as special as the silence had been. I was completely on my own and with no idea where to go. After minutes of shock, I realized that I would have to try to find my way back.

There were no signs, no lights anywhere, and my bike's light was broken. Various dirt "roads" awaited me. I'm not sure if I panicked, if I was extremely afraid, or just what my emotion was. I was in a state of disbelief.

As I set off, things only became worse since the pathways — call them roads — presented numerous choices. Bushes and trees created an even more bewildering atmosphere. There was no one anywhere, nor was a house to be seen. I continued to pedal for many minutes.

I was truly in the dark.

I have been saved several times in my life without knowing how or why. This time it was by a motorcyclist, whose faint light appeared in the distance. I don't know which of the two of us was more surprised to see the other. He stopped and asked what I was doing out on a bike at this time of night. Thankfully, he knew where my hostess lived. It was a mile away from where we were. He slowly led me home, ending one of the blackest nights of my life.

A STUDENT'S SUPPOSITION: IS YOGA LIFE?

I like to arrange yoga trips to various places, often selected for their unique beauty and power. One year the group traveled to Filicudi, a remote volcanic island thirty miles off the northeast coast of Sicily. The population of this remote island is two hundred and fifty.

A unique atmosphere of ancient history is there. The mountains are steep and rugged. When the taxi climbed up the narrow road leading to our house, we despaired over the long, challenging walk that led down to the sea. It didn't seem likely that in only a few days we would be hiking to the beach without a second thought. "Our legs become strengthened even without doing asanas," someone observed.

The sea was invitingly clear and clean. Diving into the pristine water, swimming with open eyes, I was dazzled by the aquamarine colors. I was transported into a past beyond understanding where the flux of light fascinated with its ever-changing patterns, beckoning into a world of timelessness. The rare sea scene was awe-inspiring, unexpected, and majestic. It was so unearthly that it was easy to imagine that the songs of mythical mermaids, or Sirens, as recounted in The Odyssey, must surely have come from here.

After my swim, I began the walk back home. It gave me time to think about the comments that each member of the group had made in our final week's session of breathing practice (*Pranayama*). In general, most people discover that they experience the benefits of yoga much differently after a week of practicing twice a day. In fact, the participants had discovered new aspects of themselves. I felt happy remembering their comments since they indicated a new profundity that can't really be taught, *per se*, since personal discoveries must be experienced.

These are a few of their observations:

"Emptiness isn't necessarily the absence of something. It can be filled with sounds, sensation and colors."

"To breathe with attention I have to become more disciplined because *Pranayama* implies discipline. Breath is life. Yoga involves discipline. Does that mean that yoga is life?"

"Not looking at my watch to time my breath, but rather interacting with the rustle of the palm tree above my head, made these moments magical. Could this be the secret of finding a natural exchange between my in-breath and my out-breath?"

"After a few breaths, although my eyes were closed, I began to see a hole with fretted walls that dissolved into the distance that turned into an enormous sky. I realize that yoga is the discipline that will help me become more reflective."

Across the valley the voices of the dogs and goats mingled with the cries of a child together with sounds of laughter. Beyond that could be heard the distant breaking of rough waves that over the millenniums had rolled the beach stones smooth and round. The torrid sun, the strong wind, the scarcity of water, the hours of yoga spent together, unexpectedly brought us harmony, peace, and a deeper understanding of our strengths and our fragilities.

DOORS

Doors are quite fascinating.
Almost any door you look at tells a story.
A door that is open is so inviting and so much easier to enter than a closed one.
Here are some door quotations. Each one tells a story:

It is the joy of the teachers teaching that the pupils drink,
And that very joy opens the doors through which pupils learn.
Vanda Scaravelli

Teachers open the door; but you must enter by yourself.
Chinese Proverb

Questioning is the door of knowledge.
Irish saying

May your troubles be less,
May your blessings be more,
May nothing but happiness come through your door!
Irish saying

A door—An invitation—Step in.

The door to my studio

FLOWER GRACE

Péter and I went to Bali for twelve days on our summer vacation. Every morning, I noticed that small flower offerings had been left in front of most doors. Upon inquiry, I was told that the local custom is to prepare small flower offerings to the gods. These are reverently prepared early every morning. They are offered with a prayer: a request for business when deposited in front of a shop; for safety if placed in a car; for linguistic skill in front of a tourist agency. The requests are endless in variety. The one thing that they have in common, however, is that they all ask for protection from evil spirits.

Each little square basket, ingeniously constructed by hand, is woven out of young coconut leaves. The rib of the coconut leaf is folded, and the mid-section of each one forms one side of the basket. The ribbing is carefully torn down its center, so that it has more flexibility. Additional pleasing patterns are created by bending the leaves into various shapes. The bottom is formed with two broad leaves that are perfectly flat and very wide. They are joined together by small sharp pieces of bamboo that serve as toothpicks.

Many flowers are placed inside: orange nasturtiums, blue hydrangeas, red fire-cracker hibiscus, white frangipani, magenta bougainvilleas and a very dainty, highly sought-after, fragrant, pale-yellow flower that is only found at the top of tall trees. These are only a few of the flowers that are placed in the baskets. The simple beauty of their bright colors and perfume is inspirational. This lively combination contributes to create a very unique form of prayer. Small pieces of banana, rice, or lemon may also be found in the offering.

Upon completion, a stick of incense is lit and the basket is placed on an altar, a street corner, the entrance to a building, the steps of a hotel, on walkways, or outside homes. Anywhere is appropriate because, wherever we move, we find life. Devotion is palpable and visible.

These daily offerings provide a beam of directness, a request for heavenly blessings through the humble messengers of flowers and artful handcraft. At the end of each day, having served their purpose, they finish in deterioration with the setting sun.

MORNING YOGA

It took a superhuman effort to arouse myself. My body felt heavy and sleepy, but somehow I managed to get up. I walked out onto the balcony to look at the ocean. There was so much mist that I couldn't see the water. Outside, my bare feet felt cold on the damp sand, but, nevertheless, I did my morning Tibetan prayer and, after this ritual, I was ready to do a few postures — whatever felt right for the day.

Walking along the shore, I noticed an enormous, solitary bird in the water.

There was something so daunting about its stature that it stirred a kind of fear, although, as I cautiously approached, it stayed perfectly still and proved to be quite inoffensive. Not far away, five yellow-legged birds slowly walked along the shore, hunting for the breakfast treats that each wave delivered. They tucked themselves up, slouching into their bodies, or stretched, extending their long necks, as if craning to see something.

There was great activity in the sky, which had cleared now due to the rising sun. Seagulls cried out; black pelicans, large and ominous, nose-dived into the sea and landed on their unsuspecting victims, trapping them in their enormous vice-like bills, clenching their thrashing prey, as it madly flailed in an attempt to get free.

The sea was alive with silver wavelets that were actually tiny fish, "shiners" as one fisherman called them. They were jumping out of the water in little leaps, and, as they swam, the sun caught their silver bodies, creating silver tucks in the sea. Far along the expanse of water, the shimmering forms illuminated the pale-green water like fireflies.

"Why do they jump?" I asked a fisherman. "I guess because they are nervous," he answered. That didn't seem like an altogether reasonable answer, so when I came upon another fisherman, I asked the same question. "They're trying to jump away from other fish that are trying to catch them. Everyone around here is out to get them."

Each one of us often has a different explanation of the same phenomenon, and usually, unthinkingly, we are convinced that our interpretation of a fact is the correct one.

NEW POSSIBILITIES FOR LEARNING

QUINCY JONES

Time Magazine pronounced Quincy Jones one of the most influential jazz musicians of the 20th century. His talents are endless. He has been a conductor, an arranger, a composer, a humanitarian, and an instrumentalist. His career spans six decades. At eighty-one, he still travels extensively and was recently in Italy, accompanying young musicians on tour.

In a recent interview he said, "For me the most important thing has never been money. Music must be first and exist above all other things. You must love and respect it. You have to be able to express what you feel inside; you have to touch peoples' hearts. You must be authentic. That's it.

"I have always played out of love. When you do it for money, God leaves the room."

I think there are many correlations between Quincy's "creed" and what a true yoga teacher lives and believes.

VANDA'S WISDOM

A few of Vanda's words taken from my notes of our lessons together.

"You don't need me. Dig in, you will find all of the answers."

"When there is no resistance, everything works out."

We were practicing the vibrating Om (a breathing practice) and she said: "Don't waste energy singing — vibrate — as soon as you relax, it vibrates. It's as if you play the body."

One day when I was practicing backbends, in desperation I said: "It is so slow." She replied: "Do you realize what you are doing? It is a miraculous kind of thing. Spinal fluid is moving from the sacrum up to the brain." Another time I complained and said: "Why can't I go down?" and she said: "Because you don't go up enough. It is like a ball. The harder you bounce it down, the higher it goes up. It is anti-gravity."

Often she would have me breathe on the edge of two walls that form an angle. The back of my waist touched the edge where the two walls met (but my head was not to touch it). By touching the edge in this way, the lungs relax. She said: "I don't know how it happens."

While practicing the standing positions: "I am absolutely sure that this is right. The Egyptians did it as did the Etruscans, but then it got lost."

"When I die, you must be able to carry this on." Her tone was as matter as fact as "pass me a spoon" while we were having lunch together.

To one of my students, a famous professor of Art History: "Have the courage to be mediocre. There is nothing that is special. When you think you are special, it's a sure sign that you're not."

"Your body can always answer the question." I said: "Mine doesn't," and she answered: "That's because you're too busy asking and not listening to the answer."

When she asked if I was doing what it was that she was teaching me, I said: "not really," and she replied, "That's all right. First your mind understands it, and then the rest will follow."

A comment about putting weight on the heels: "It is so simple that no one understands it. If it were complicated, everyone would get it right away!"

"Bodies are so intelligent. Once you understand, the body will do it because it likes it."

"Relax. But not relax, sleeping. Relax means to be intensely alert to what happens inside you. It is important. To be aware, to be awake, not to sleep. To be attentive, to be conscious."

*Vanda using her bodily weight, fists and knees to
remind me of specific points to activate.
Her feet and toes, too, are fully engaged in this process.*

SMALL THINGS

For in the dew of little things, the heart finds its morning and is refreshed.
Kahlil Gibran

Alberta, my painter friend, was telling me about the difficulty of drawing something very small as opposed to something very large. Painting a tiny vase and getting the details right takes innumerable skills. Not only does it involve the hand, but it also takes "character" skills such as patience, courage, perseverance, etc.

My thoughts turned to yoga. Some asanas need to be repeated hundreds of times. It takes great patience and perseverance to continue to practice in spite of never succeeding to do a position "correctly." I have tried some positions thousands of times but still have not been able to do them the way I had hoped. Courage is also needed, because some movements are very difficult. And paying attention to very small movements can be an oasis that replenishes the body and soul.

Even if we are not artists, remembering the importance of "character skills" may add meaning to our daily lives. We can practice observing small, everyday things. This is the art of living life. It is not always the grandiose moments that count, for they will only come from time to time. Rather, the small moments have value, and, if we pay attention to them and accept their worth, they can add to the richness that life offers us.

FOOD FOR THOUGHT

Food prepared with loving care and attention can communicate more than many nice words. It can even be more curative than medicine. In fact, various cultures have a special food that is given to sick people. Often it has the power to make a person feel considerably better.

You may be asking, "What has this to do with yoga?" How can preparing a meal have anything to do with it? Does it take special focus to pay attention to what you are preparing? (How many times have you, like me, burned something or overcooked it, having forgotten about its being on the stove or in the oven?) Can you put love or your mantra into the food? Does it make a difference if you are angry while cooking? Will practicing mindful breathing be helpful if you are preparing something in the kitchen?

Offering a person something as simple as a nutritious slice of lightly toasted bread with extra virgin olive oil, a swipe of garlic, finely chopped tomatoes and basil (something we love in Italy), can be as appealing as a three-course meal. A bowl of spaghetti is the ultimate comfort food for many of us. It can cheer a person up.

Our yoga practice can help us when we cook for ourselves and others, once we have realized the magic of food that has been properly prepared.

BREATHING COLORS

This is an exercise in which you visualize different colors and then unite them with your breath. It can help you to find out where energy may have gotten stuck. It offers an opportunity to reawaken some areas of your mind that have been dormant. It is potent and gentle at the same time.

A color and your breath meet together in a specific zone or chakra. Most probably you will find that some colors are more difficult to visualize. Linger and "bathe" in them as long as you want to.

Sit cross-legged or in any other position. Close your eyes and get in touch with your breath.

1. Visualize **RED** at the very base of your spine. Spend some time breathing with the color red in that area. When you are able to " breath with it," then move on to:

2. **ORANGE** Direct your attention to the sacrum. Breathe with curiosity as you visualize orange. Do not be in a hurry. When your breath and the color are united, proceed to:

3. **YELLOW** Locate the solar plexus, and place your hands on your abdomen. Get involved with a bright yellow color and enjoy it and the sensation of warmth produced by your breathing.

Now combine the three colors. Start from the bottom and inhale red, progressing to orange and then to yellow. Exhale "from the top," going from **yellow** through **orange** to **red**. Continue doing this for a while. The colors and the breath will flow from one to the other. When this sensation becomes fluid, proceed to:

4. **GREEN** in the heart area (which is nestled between your lungs)
Stay focused on your esoteric heart.
Green, green, green.
Breathe, breathe, breathe.

When you are comfortable with green in this area, you may lightly move down through all the preceding colors as you exhale. It is a bit like being in a delicate fountain. Allow the inhalation to do what it will.
Move on to:

5. **BLUE** in the area of your throat. Dwell only on blue. I think you will find this interesting, as it is not a small area. The repercussions are enormous. Stay centered there. Almost as an afterthought, you can lightly move down through the other colors following the same procedure as before during exhalation. Then go directly to:

6. **INDIGO** in the center of your forehead. Unite color and breath in this center. Take some time and "live" in this space for a while. It might change if you remain very relaxed and open.

In the same way that you united **red**, **orange**, and **yellow**, now unite **green**, **blue** and **indigo**.

From here, go directly to:

7. **VIOLET** at the very top of your head (at exactly the point that touches the ground when you stand on your head). It is the crown, "the thousand petaled lotus," which you now inundate with violet and breath.

You, the lotus, must continue to keep your roots in the earth to maintain blossoms (thus visualize your connection to red). At this point you may begin to experience that all of the colors are connected and that they flow into each other.

As you breathe, inhale the colors starting from **red** and proceeding through **orange**, **yellow**, **green**, **blue**, and **indigo** to **violet**.

And then sweetly exhale from violet through the colors back to red.

Continue to go up and down.

Do not be "grabby" about your inhalation. Let it come to you.

MARIO – DIGNITY AND HARD WORK

Many Italians drink bottled water, as our city water comes from the Arno River. Our water in the country is piped through more than five hundred meters of plastic tubing, and so out of necessity, we need to drink bottled water. I refuse, however, to buy water in plastic bottles, and so I have glass bottles delivered to our house.

The water comes in a heavy crate that holds twelve bottles. It needs to be carried by hand down a very steep driveway and then hauled through a long corridor so we can store it in an inconvenient closet. Mario, our deliveryman, is well over fifty and is neither tall nor hefty but the difficulty of his work does not seem to faze him. He is also extremely courteous and cheerful and never complains about the effort. I look forward to seeing him every time he comes.

One summer, in the middle of a heat wave, Mario arrived at the very hottest time of the day. He happily unloaded his truck and carried two crates at a time. I have offered coffee, water, or a drink to Mario many times but he has always refused, but on this particularly sweltering day he was willing to stop to chat for a few minutes.

He told me he had taken the commuter train at six in the morning, adding two hours to his eight-hour day. I said I thought he must be exhausted at the end of the day and expected that he would grumble about the disadvantage of living far away from his job.

"Oh, no," he told me, "I am not tired when I get home. I love to go out into the garden at the end of my day. My father was a farmer, and I have inherited his love for the land. It is true that tilling the soil is physically demanding, but I am sure I stay healthier by doing so. The entire time I am in my garden, I am happy and carefree."

Mario is a yogi in action. He does his job perfectly and is untouched by the whims of the weather or how he is treated by others. He is balanced and constant, and his work is perfect. He is nurtured from a motor within that he keeps in tune by being in touch with the earth and his deeper self.

UNANSWERED QUESTIONS

THE HOW OF WHY

There comes a time when we are forced to ask ourselves hard questions. Among the most difficult are "Why are we alive?" and "What are we living for?" Usually these questions are brutally forced upon us at the death of a friend, because of some calamity, or when we face a serious illness.

It seems to me that a possible way to make sense out of life is to look at each day as if it were a life in itself. At the end of every day, we might ask ourselves if we feel ready and could be at peace with ourselves if we should die at that moment. In other words, have we lived the day mindfully? Has it been acceptable? How did we do? Recently, I heard the Dalai Lama comment on how he approached these questions. He said that, every morning upon getting up, he inquired into his activities of the previous day.

Learning to appreciate the beauty within the small enriching moments of our lives is helpful. A child's sweet voice, a smile given to or received from a stranger, a meal eaten in peace, a gratifying run, a courtesy offered to another driver, a thank you to a cashier or clerk, any event can offer nourishment.

When there are dark days and despair, perhaps these kinds of spiritual comfort seem inadequate. But there is still the strength of the breath.

Focusing the mind on breathing can change our mental outlook. The first step is to realize that we are breathing. Then we need to pay attention to the lungs when they are filling with new air that should enter in a very relaxed way, without being pulled. After some minutes, there will be an almost imperceptible sound as the air enters. Simply listening to this sound can take us to a safe place. The sound is reminiscent of that of the sea, which can be very comforting. In certain circumstances this might be one of the few resources we have. There is a deep archaic recognition that touches us; it is stored within our bodies, and it is available to all of us. It is healing and can carry us far far away into "green pastures."

The "why" is a mystery many have tried to answer

There are other ways to shield oneself from discouragement. Without any particular mental effort on our part, the long-forgotten words of wisdom from a grandparent or childhood friend may suddenly come to mind. Those simple thoughts—perhaps things that we heard repeated often in the past—may open a window for us. We don't know how or why these helpful messages arrive, but they are there. They are life preservers thrown out to save us when we are floundering.

We can remember the small things, not the large ones. Let us leave the grand explanations to the giants of this earth. The "why" part is a mystery that many have tried to answer. It is the "how" part over which we have control. The list of "hows" is infinite and challenging, but, if we can remind ourselves of some of the small gifts that life offers, perhaps we can find hope and improve the way we live our days.

A PRICELESS RESOURCE

One can live for some time without food and water, but one cannot live without air. Most people, even yoga students, fail to think sufficiently about their breathing habits. It is a constant learning process to educate the mind to remain relaxed, with the body alert, and watch the breath at the same time. A great yogi observed that the breath is harder to train than a lion. This wisdom encourages me and helps on those days when nothing in my practice seems to be working. It is through attention to the breath—the very essence of yoga—that health, mind, and spirits are improved.

Students often want to know which position is the best for practicing *Pranayama*, (breathing exercises). One needs to be as comfortable as possible. *Vajarasana* (sitting on heels), sitting with legs crossed simply, or *Padmasana* (the lotus pose) are all very acceptable. One should never put oneself into a position that is painful and impedes relaxation. Holding an uncomfortable position can easily make one want to give up; nonetheless, the back should be as straight as possible. When there are stiff knees or a sore back, sitting on a chair or a low bench is a better choice. Yoga is for everyone and should be encouraged even for those confined to bed rest or in any difficult situation.

Someone once said in class: "I get distracted when I begin to breathe. I can watch my inhalation and exhalation a few times but then the busy thinking mind takes over. This is a constant problem every time I practice *Pranayama*. My mind strays and thoughts often turn into worries. What can I do?"

Begin by watching and accepting your unsolicited thoughts with kindness and curiosity. Try not to dwell on them and to consider them non-judgmentally. Then bring your mind back to observing the breath. Remember that thoughts can get washed away with fresh breaths. You have a new chance after the end of each exhalation because it is a new beginning.

As you exhale, follow the air through your lungs. The area from the waist down to the last vertebra of the sacrum can release towards the floor. As this occurs, the whole upper part of your body becomes lighter and it slowly opens. The out-flowing breath empties your lungs and opens your chest at the same time. At the end of each exhalation, relax and allow the incoming breath to satiate you with new air. The more you become a detached observer as you absorb the air, the more satisfying the whole process becomes. Remember that breath control is a very demanding process and that managing to control the breath for even a short period of time is an excellent achievement.

As I sit and breathe, sometimes I can hear the rhythmical sound of my breath as it flows in and out through my nostrils. It reminds me of the sound of gentle waves lapping on the shore. As I inhale, I have a sense of a little wave swelling and beginning to reach the shore. Exhalation is the wave receding back into the vast ocean. It is no wonder, therefore, that paying attention to this natural music has a calming effect. It opens a window towards space and purity. I cannot direct the movements, and I must surrender to something much greater than myself. As a sea shell held to your ear echoes the sound of the sea, so too your ever-present breath is there to soothe and replenish.

As a seashell echoes the sound of the sea, your ever-present breath soothes and replenishes.

THE GOD WHO TREASURES THE LESS THAN PERFECT

There is a special God who has a holy place where all of our not quite perfect things are happily received and remembered; the pie that burnt a bit, the piece of sewing where the seams weren't perfect, the car that in spite of being washed still had dirty spots, the yoga position that didn't come out right.

Dedicate these acts to the One, who is like a loving mother with many children and is used to the varying conditions of the human lot, and who loves each child in the absent-minded way of one who cares for many. The One will appreciate your less than perfect offering.

Why do we always think that only perfection has value?

THE TURTLE DILEMMA

I never expected to participate in the birth of a sea turtle. As I walked along the beach in Florida, I was drawn to a large area that was sectioned off with yellow tape. My heart jumped when I saw movement in the sand and discerned a tiny sea turtle scratching his way out of its egg and beginning his long, torturous walk across the sand to continue his life in the water. The incubation period had ended, the moon was waning, and the call to the sea beckoned hundreds of new-born turtles. It was as difficult a process as any birth. The trek was demanding, and uncertain. As the minutes passed, this tiny creature rested more and more often, almost puffing with exhaustion.

I dared not touch him, as I felt restrained by the knowledge that many newborn animals must not be interfered with. I reasoned that this struggle was necessary to strengthen the muscles needed in life, so I stood, awestruck, beside this tiny creature, touched by the role that nature had offered me as an observer.

It was such a long trek! How did he know which direction to take? His skin was becoming whitish and his stops for rest were longer and more frequent. He seemed to be getting closer to death than to life.

The arrival of a local resident changed everything. He confidently picked up the baby turtle and took it to the ocean. "If they get too exhausted, they don't have the energy to swim through the waves to get out into open water." The little turtle rolled over in the waves and was brought back to shore, unable to get out into deep water. It seemed he was going to perish.

His savior walked into the water and picked him up once more to take him beyond the waves. "He will come up for air three times and then understand how to move." The turtle surfaced, took in air, then went down to the floor of the ocean. There was a long wait before he surfaced for air once again. The waves rocked, but this time the turtle was able to surface for the last time. His little black shell disappeared as he dove in the waves. His long journey towards full development had begun.

I contemplated my policy of non-intervention. I had thought I was doing the right thing by not interfering, but my incorrect assumption would have led to the death of the turtle.

The interminable trek to the sea

ACKNOWLEDGEMENTS

To Vanda:
Who never leaves me and remains a beacon forever.
She is an incomparable role model for all teachers.

I owe the successful completion of my book to dear ones who have offered me their enormous talents, help, and support. Overflowing gratitude and thanks to the following people:

Wallis Wilde Menozzi, life-long friend, for her poet's ear, writer's sensitivity, steady confidence, and gentle prodding. She is an unparalleled international author who remains to be discovered by many.

Lydia Greenfield, the first person to believe that I really would accomplish writing this book by sending me her magnificent drawings over the years. What an honor to have such a talented artist represent my words through her drawings.

Constance Dilley, who enthusiastically trimmed, patched, and improved spots that confounded me.

Rab Hatfield, brilliant author and art historian, for his thoughtful and outstanding corrections. Thirty years of studying yoga with me helped him to decipher passages that were unclear.

Dorothea Barrett, whose impeccable editorial craftsmanship added the perfect finishing touch.

Paola Scaravelli Cohen for her kind permission to use quotations from *Awakening the Spine* (Pinter and Martin Ltd., 2012 edition) and for encouraging me to continue writing.

Helen Noakes, yoga companion and sometime photographer.

Laura Hayhurst for her inspiring photo illustrating "The Ocean Garden."

Anna and **Stephen Wolfenden** for permission to include "Rebecca at Her Bakery."

Francesca Casciarri, whose companionship on the set of "La Fuga" was a joy.

Cristiano Papi for the hours we spent together at the computer. His good humor throughout the many revisions was welcome.

Francesco Filippini. His unrelenting computer hand and eye saved my many mix-ups.

Roberto Gigli. His expert draftmanship and advice brought *bellezza* to these pages.

To my family:

Michele for being the first person to read and approve of the manuscript and for encouraging me by listening.

Alessandra for her talent to see correspondences between seemingly unrelated essays and finding an order and rhythm to them.

Péter whose patience was greatly appreciated.

ILLUSTRATIONS

Page 10   Laura Hayhurst, Agonda Beach, Goa: 2016.
Page 15   Helen Noakes, Jibhi, India: 2016.
Page 17   Lydia Greenfield, pen, ink and ink wash, Serpiolle, Italy: 2004.
Page 19   www.pixabay.com
Page 21   www.florencescaravelli.com
Page 24   Author unknown, Castiglione della Pescaia, Italy: 2013
Page 25   Francesca Casciarri, (Perché No Film production) Rome Italy: 2015
Page 33   Lydia Greenfield, pen, ink and ink wash, Serpiolle, Italy: 2004.
Page 35   Elizabeth Lutz Pauncz (ELP), Cleveland, Ohio: 1950.
Page 37   Lydia Greenfield, pen, ink and ink wash, Serpiolle, Italy: 1997.
Page 41   ELP, Sarasota, Florida: 2018.
Page 44   Lydia Greenfield, pen, ink and ink wash, Serpiolle, Italy: 2005.
Page 47   Lydia Greenfield, pen, ink and ink wash, Serpiolle, Italy: 2011.
Page 49   Lydia Greenfield, pen, ink and ink drawing, Serpiolle, Italy: 1994.
Page 51   Lydia Greenfield, pen, ink and ink drawing, Australia: 2006.
Page 53   Dario Andreozzi, Castiglione della Pescaia, Italy: 2013.
Page 56   ELP, Budapest, Hungary: 2017.
Page 57   Rosella Baroncini, (with her kind permission), place and date unknown.
Page 59   Anna and Stephen Wolfenden, East Suffolk, England: 2016.
Page 63   Anon, www.pixabay.com
Page 67   Helen Noakes, Rishikesh, India: 2016.
Page 69   ELP, Auroville, India: 2007.
Page 74   ELP, Florence, Italy: 2018.

Page 76   Anon, www.pixabay.com
Page 78   ELP, Sarasota, Florida: 2016.
Page 80   Anon, www.pixabay.com
Page 83   Arturo Patten/Archives IMEC, (with kind permission), Florence, Italy: 1990
Page 85   Anon, www.pixabay.com
Page 93   Lydia Greenfield, pen, ink and ink drawing, Tuscany, Italy: 2012.
Page 97   Anon, www.pixabay.com
Page 100 Lydia Greenfield, pen, ink and ink drawing, Sarasota, Florida: 2016.

ABOUT THE AUTHOR

Elizabeth began her yoga studies at the Light of Yoga Society in 1972, when she and her family were on vacation in Cleveland. Returning to Florence, Italy, she trained alone for two years on her own and continued for a further ten years of study with Dona Holleman. This work culminated in a month's stay in Pune, India, at the Ramamani Iyengar Memorial Institute. Subsequently, she became a private student of Vanda Scaravelli. The twelve years spent with Scaravelli radically changed and enriched Elizabeth's understanding and practice of yoga.

For Elizabeth, travel and yoga are deeply connected. Among her most memorable travels is a journey to Vietnam with Thich Nhat Hanh as a member of his peace delegation. She has also led groups to special places of power throughout Italy and in various other countries, such as Greece, Morocco, Egypt, and India. Her studio in Florence has welcomed students since 1991.

Elizabeth Lutz Pauncz was born and raised in Cleveland, Ohio. She graduated from the University of Michigan and then moved to Italy, where she married, raised a family, worked, and received another degree from the University of Florence.

Elizabeth can be contacted at

New Yoga Center
Via Puccinotti 15
Florence, 50129
Italy.
Website: www.florencescaravelli.com
E-mail: florencescaravelli@gmail.com

Books by the author may be purchased directly by contacting her e-mail address:

Elizabeth Lutz Pauncz, *The Egyptian Sun Salutation and Yoga*, M.I.R. Edizioni, 1998

Elizabeth Lutz Pauncz, *Seven Days of Relaxing Practice*, a bound photocopied manual.

DVDs

Elizabeth Lutz Pauncz, *Remembering Vanda*: the DVD was made in India, in collaboration with Helen Noakes, and can be ordered at https://www.helennoakes.net/shop/; in it, many postures are demonstrated and explained by Elizabeth.

Elizabeth Lutz Pauncz, *Vanda's Yoga and Elizabeth's Reflections*. The DVD contains twenty-two minutes of Vanda Scaravelli doing yoga, with commentary by Elizabeth, followed by Elizabeth demonstrating and explaining Vanda's three cornerstones: "breath" (at the Etruscan amphitheater at Fiesole), "wave" (at Elizabeth's studio in Florence) and "gravity" (at Vanda's garden in Fiesole). This is the only video in existence of Vanda practicing. A hard copy can be ordered by contacting Elizabeth directly. Downloading may be done by reaching https://www.florencescaravelli.com

Finished printing – July 2019

Printed in Poland
by Amazon Fulfillment
Poland Sp. z o.o., Wrocław